The Empty Birdfeeder

Written by
Theresa Wyatt

Illustrated by
Mick McArt

MICK ART
PRODUCTIONS LLC
PUBLISHING

This is a work of fiction. Except in references to the Lord Jesus Christ, the events and characters described herein are imaginary and not intended to refer to specific places or living persons. The author has represented and warranted full ownership and/or legal right to publish all the materials in this book.

The Empty Birdfeeder
All Rights Reserved
Copyright © 2012 Theresa Wyatt
V1.0

This book may not be reproduced, transmitted, or stored in whole or in part by any means, including graphics, electronic, or mechanical without the express written consent of the publisher except in the case of brief quotations embodied in critical articles and reviews.

ISBN: 978-0-9827000-6-8
LCCN: 2012944308

Published by
Mick Art Productions, LLC
www.mickartproductions.com

PRINTED IN THE UNITED STATES OF AMERICA

Do not be anxious about anything, but in everything, by prayer and petition, with thanksgiving, present your requests to God. And the peace of God which transcends all understanding will guard your hearts and your mind in Christ Jesus.
Philippians 4: 6-7

Nestled by a small quiet town was a beautiful park. This park was special. Birds traveled hundreds of miles to visit this park as they migrated north or south. Many of these birds made a habit of visiting the yards near the park, including the backyard of a little boy named Jonathon.

Now Jonathon loved God very much. He understood God made the world and everything in it. Although he loved all of God's creatures, Jonathon was especially fond of the many birds that gathered in his yard. On any given day, there were blue jays, robins, red winged blackbirds, sparrows and his favorite, chickadees.

Jonathon had many bird feeders in his yard. He would go out every day to fill them with fresh seed and place fresh fruit slices in the sides for the orioles. Sometimes, he would sit in his favorite chair and talk to the birds as they ate. "You are special", "Did you know that God made you and me", "I love you"; Jonathon could be heard saying to them. The many birds would sing to Jonathon in return.

Jonathon fed his birds in all kinds of weather. He fed them on sunny days. He fed them when it was very windy and when it rained. He even fed them in the deepest of snow of a winters' day. "Here is a special treat", Jonathon would tell them as he placed suet on the sides of the bird feeder. "This will keep you warm".

One spring day while Jonathon was filling one of his feeders, he heard a strange noise. Hiding in the grass was a baby robin. The little robin looked up at Jonathon and shivered. Jonathon could tell he was frightened. "Well now, how did you get way down here?" Jonathon spoke softly as he looked around. The baby robin's parents were not nearby to help him. Carefully, Jonathon pulled his favorite chair over by the baby robin and sat with him. "We will wait together for your mom and dad to come home", Jonathon said. "Everything will be ok", he said trying to comfort the baby bird. They waited and waited.

Hours had gone by, but the baby robin's parents had not yet returned home. Jonathon held the baby bird in his hand and prayed for the safe return of his parents. Jonathon knew God was faithful to prayers and taught the little robin all about God while they waited. "God made you and me and he loves us very much", Jonathon explained. "When we are lost and frightened, we should pray and tell Jesus what is in our heart. He wants us to come to Him for help".

A short time later, the little robin's parents returned home. At first they were frightened of Jonathon. But he spoke gently to them and they seemed to understand he had watched over their baby.

Before dinner, Jonathon's dad came home and helped place the baby back inside the nest. Mr. & Mrs. Robin began singing. "They seem happy, don't they dad?" Jonathon asked. "Maybe they're thanking God for keeping their baby safe".

Smiling, Jonathon's dad said, "Maybe they are also thanking God for the little boy who cared for their baby".

After this, Mr. & Mrs. Robin would sing to Jonathon outside his bedroom window every morning as he woke. Jonathon would jump out bed and hurry to the window, "Good morning to you!!" He would say.

One evening, the birds came to visit one of Jonathon's feeders. It was empty!! In fact, all of the feeders were empty. There wasn't even a smidgen of fruit to be found. SOMETHING WAS WRONG! Jonathon never forgot to feed them.

Mr. & Mrs. Robin immediately flew over to the maple tree just outside Jonathon's bedroom window. The baby robin was close behind. As they peeked inside, there was little Jonathon lying in his bed. His mother was sitting beside him. She was heard praying to Jesus for Jonathon to get better. "Please Jesus, heal my little boy", she whispered.

By now many of the birds were gathered in the maple tree outside Jonathon's bedroom window. All at once, the birds began to chatter. Puzzled, Jonathon's mom watched from the window and wondered what they could be saying.

All through the night the birds kept watch, as Jonathon's mother prayed. Just as the sun began to peek over the horizon, the birds began singing, very softly, with the beautiful voices that God gave them – and Jonathon loved so much.

Jonathon lay very still in his bed. All at once, his eyes began to flutter! His eyes popped open and he sat up with a big smile. "My birds are singing for me momma, isn't it lovely?" "Yes, Jonathon, their voices are beautiful", his mother replied with tears in her eyes. As Jonathon got out of bed to look out the window, the birds sang louder.

"Momma, do you think they are singing to God?" Yes, I do Jonathon. Do you remember the verse daddy taught you?" "OH, yes!" Jonathon said excitedly. "Let everything that hath breath praise the Lord! Praise ye the Lord!"

Jonathon's little friends watched all day as he got stronger. The next morning, the birds awoke to the sound of fresh seed being poured into their feeders. On the sides were fresh orange slices glistening in the morning sun. Jonathon sat in his favorite chair and watched as the birds ate joyfully. He couldn't help but smile as they sang. He was happy to be alive. He loved all of God's creatures, but there was a special place in his heart for birds.

The End

Theresa Wyatt
Author

This story was inspired by a baby robin my son found in our backyard. God used this situation as a seed to this story. The journey of writing and publishing this book has involved many lessons of obedience and patience for me. As I write this I am aware acutely aware that I can do all things through Christ which strengtheneth me Philippians 4:13.

Theresa lives in Croswell Michigan with her husband and children.
She is a nurse and is currently working on her PhD in Nursing.

Mick McArt
Illustrator

Mick McArt was raised in Tawas, Michigan and was a young man when he gave his heart to the Lord. He sees his imagination as a gift from God and hopes to use it to encourage other Christian artists. With encouragement from his wife, pastor, and friends, Mick began work on the Tales of Wordishure Christian children's book series in 2009. Shortly after publishing his own material he started Mick Art Productions Publishing to help promote other Christian authors.

He currently attends Faith Baptist Church, in Saginaw, Michigan. There he met and married his wife Erica. They currently live in Saginaw with their son Micah. Mick earned a Bachelor of Fine Arts degree from Central Michigan University and a Masters degree from Saginaw Valley State University.

The opportunity to work with Theresa Wyatt on this book, not only as her publisher, but as the illustrator was a fun blessing. To learn more about Mick McArt go to:
www.mickartproductions.com

MICK ART PRODUCTIONS LLC
PUBLISHING

Other Christian books available from
Mick Art Productions Publishing:

By Mick McArt:
Tales of Wordishure: Book I
Tales of Wordishure: Book II
The Silent Knight of Wordishure
Songs of Wordishure Music CD
(Children's)

Casey Brand New by Jan Lord
(Children's)

Redeemed by Charles C. Smith
(Poetry)

Night of Destiny by Kelly Ann Reed
(Historical Romance)

All books are available at:
www.mickartproductions.com

www.ingramcontent.com/pod-product-compliance
Lightning Source LLC
Chambersburg PA
CBHW081352040426
42450CB00015B/3405